The Prodigal Parent

The Prodigal Parent

It's Never Too Late (And They're Never Too Old)
To Reach Your Children with the Gospel!

EJ RICHARDS

XULON PRESS

Xulon Press
2301 Lucien Way #415
Maitland, FL 32751
407.339.4217
www.xulonpress.com

© 2021 by EJ Richards

Edited by Debra Glagola

All rights reserved solely by the author. The author guarantees all contents are original and do not infringe upon the legal rights of any other person or work. No part of this book may be reproduced in any form without the permission of the author. The views expressed in this book are not necessarily those of the publisher.

Unless otherwise indicated, Scripture quotations taken from the New King James Version (NKJV). Copyright © 1982 by Thomas Nelson, Inc. Used by permission. All rights reserved.

Printed in the United States of America

Paperback ISBN-13: 9781662813030
Ebook ISBN-13: 9781662813047

Table of Contents

Dedication vi
Foreword xi
Preface xv
Introduction xix
The Most Important Things xxvi
God 1
Jesus 10
Holy Spirit 19
The Bible 30
Faith 38
Prayer 49
Salvation 61
The Church 76
The Cross 88
The Resurrection 104
End Matters 117

Dedication

THIS BOOK IS DEDICATED TO TIFFANY

MY WONDERFUL DAUGHTER

I LOVE YOU AND THANK GOD FOR YOU!

Dedication

Acknowledgements

I would like to thank and acknowledge Rev. Dr. Christopher Alan Bullock, Dr. Debbie Bullock, the ministers, deacons and all the saints of God at Canaan Baptist Church in New Castle Delaware. I acknowledge your love and fellowship and I thank you for all the prayers and support. I praise and thank God for all of you.

> *Behold, how good and how pleasant it is for brethren to dwell together in unity! Psalms 133:1*

The Prodigal Parent

I would like to thank my beautiful wife Maudette who's enduring and bountiful love continues to be the blessing that the Bible speaks of when it says -

> ***He who finds a wife finds a good thing, And obtains favor from the LORD. Proverbs 18:22***

Foreword

Every so often we are blessed to meet individuals whose unique relationship with God allows for unusual insight into the Scriptures and their application to the human predication. One such person is EJ Richards, Coast Guard Academy graduate, retired president of a fortune 100 company, Founder, President EA Enterprises USA, and a preacher and teacher of God's Word. How blessed we are to have in print the roadmap of one whose theology demonstrates what Christian ministry ought to be as we make our way through these trying, uncertain, and stressful times.

There were struggles and difficulties that EJ was able to get through only by the love and grace of God. But he does not speak of, suggest, or imply in any way that the struggles in his life contributed to his being a "Prodigal Parent". His entire focus is enlightening others to the reality of God being present with us in all situations. These are disturbing and challenging times in this country, with a plethora of traps and detractors that will ensnare the unprepared and ill-informed. The allure of materialism, greed, and a cult following that worships the anti-christ of the age is rampant. Life is hard! Covid-19, cancer in our bodies, broken relationships, suicide, gambling, domestic violence, and drugs are real! There is trouble on all fronts.

But we can overcome the fears that grip us in this new era. Love, contentment, and restoration can be found. God can take what was meant for evil and turn it around into good. He is the same yesterday, today, and forever more. People and the systems

Foreword

of this world will fail you. Put your trust and faith in God. Rev. Richards' determination and unshakable faith in God comes through loud and clear not only for his daughter but for all of us. We need a close relationship with God to survive! I recommend "The Prodigal Parent" to everyone. It is a blueprint for all who seek guidance, understanding, comfort and a personal relationship with Jesus Christ.

Rev. Dr. Herbert J. Carey
To God Be The Glory House Of Worship
Kent, Washington

Preface

Prodigal – *one who wastes his means by indulgence.*

The Prodigal Parent, through and by the grace of God, returns to his children to restore what was wasted. Praise God for His everlasting love, His wondrous mercies, and His magnificent kindness and forgiveness. Because of Him, it is never too late.

I was sitting in church one Sunday, reflecting on statements that were spoken by the pastor about his life and his walk with God. In telling of his relationship with the Lord, it was clear that he had been blessed with knowing Jesus most of his life and had been "caught up in the church" at a very young age. His relationship with his wife is centered on the church as she is a pastor's daughter. He has two sons who are now grown; they started lives of their own and have blessed the pastor with grandchildren. I was struck by the contrast between his life and the lives of those of us who did not have that experience. In fact, some of us have traveled roads that greatly deviate from the path of this pastor.

I write this book for those people. More specifically, I write it for them and their children. While I was sitting in the church, the thought hit me so strongly that not all of us have done it "right." Many of us have squandered opportunities; it is only later in life that we realized all the things that we should have, would have, and could have taught our children. I feel in my spirit that there are so many men and women who would love to have the opportunity to do it

Preface

over again regarding how they communicated Christ—if they even communicated Christ to their children.

"It is never too late," I heard in my spirit! I believe this book will help many adult Christians tell their sons and daughters (and grandchildren, nieces, and nephews) what they wish they would have said when the children were still under their roofs. In some cases, parents may still have that opportunity.

The book goes straight to what is important. It emphasizes the urgency of knowing Jesus Christ as Lord and makes no apologies for imploring the reader to know Jesus. Why wouldn't the book take that path? As one who once was blind but now can see, it only makes sense that a parent who has now been enlightened would tirelessly and ceaselessly communicate the goodness of God, the need of the Savior, and the way of salvation.

I started writing this book for my daughter, and I dedicate it to her. I wanted to hand her something from me that said, "You can trust me when I tell you that Jesus is real and that you must be born again—and oh, yeah, I missed it by not equipping you before, but I won't let this opportunity pass me by again!" I wanted to put something in her hands that would point her to the Word of God, something she could open up like an index of the things I wish I would have taught her and shown her (demonstrated for her) when she was younger.

It is never too late.

Introduction

The Most Important Things
I Never Taught You

This is to you, my beloved child, whom I love with a forever love. You I cherish; you are constantly in my thoughts and prayers. I tremble at the thought of you not standing right in Christ. I do not say this as a judgment; rather, I say this to be sure you understand just how concerned I am about your eternal security. I plead with you with the love that is within me to understand the following Scripture and hold it close to you, so close that you keep it in mind daily to measure all your striving and efforts in life:

Matthew 6:33 *"But seek first the kingdom of God and His righteousness, and all these things shall be added to you."*

The things I am writing to you within these pages are right on time but way overdue. They are right on time because they are happening now, but they are way overdue because I should have taught you about them when you were a child. The Bible reminds us:

2 Peter 3:8 *But, beloved, do not forget this one thing, that with the Lord one day is as a thousand years, and a thousand years as one day.*

In the words of John Legend:

As I look back on all that I've done to you

Introduction

My biggest regrets, the things
that I never could do
I see the light now...

I see the light.

A far cry mine!

2 Corinthians 4:6 *For it is the God who commanded light to shine out of darkness, who has shone in our hearts to give the light of the knowledge of the glory of God in the face of Jesus Christ.*

The face of Jesus Christ—what face are we talking about? Is it the face of the bruised and beaten Savior that many people see when they think about Jesus? Probably not.

That face probably does not appear in your mind when you think of Jesus. However, to really know Him, you must look at that face: bruised, wounded, and torn. That face expresses the pain of one who has suffered terrible beatings and then death. Jesus did not deserve death, but He endured it for our sins—my sins and your sins.

Only when we understand that face—when the light shines on that face—will we fully know the face of Jesus.

> **Isaiah 53:2-6**
> *For He shall grow up before Him as a tender plant,*
> *And as a root out of dry ground.*
> *He has no form or comeliness;*
> *And when we see Him,*
> *There is no beauty that we should desire Him.*
> *He is despised and rejected by men,*
> *A Man of sorrows and acquainted with grief.*
> *And we hid, as it were, our faces from Him;*

Introduction

He was despised, and we did not esteem Him.
Surely He has borne our griefs
And carried our sorrows;
Yet we esteemed Him stricken,
Smitten by God, and afflicted.
<u>But He was wounded for our transgressions,</u>
<u>He was bruised for our iniquities;</u>
<u>The chastisement for our peace was upon Him,</u>
<u>And by His stripes we are healed.</u>
<u>All we like sheep have gone astray;</u>
<u>We have turned, every one, to his own way;</u>
<u>And the Lord has laid on Him the iniquity of us all.</u>

Yes, my dear one, all that I write to you is about knowing Jesus Christ and His fulfillment of the promises of God.

These next words from the Bible are some of the most important words I could have and should have ever said to you:

> **Romans 10:9-10** . . .*that if you confess with your mouth the Lord Jesus and believe in your heart that God has raised Him from the dead, you will be saved. For with the heart one believes unto righteousness, and with the mouth confession is made unto salvation.*

Believe and confess; there it is, dear one. When our hearts have been pricked by the Gospel of Jesus Christ, we have the opportunity to accept God's invitation to become born again.

The Prodigal Parent realizes the many things, or rather the main things, that should have been taught to you were not.

Introduction

My love for you was then and is now real and true. You are so very precious to me! However, there were things I never could do. The reason I could not do those things is because I did not see the light. But now, because of the goodness, mercy, and grace of God, I have this opportunity to tell you those things—the things I should have already told you.

As you read through these pages, I want you to know I am praying for you. I believe the God of all mercy will speak to your heart and that you will now know **The Most Important Things I Should Have Taught You**.

The Most Important Things:

1. God

2. Jesus

3. Holy Spirit

4. The Bible

5. Faith

6. Prayer

7. Salvation

8. The Church

9. The Cross

10. The Resurrection

God

The Bible teaches us who God is. My favorite Scripture in describing God is actually taken from a prayer:

> **Acts 4:24** *So when they heard that, they raised their voice to God with one accord and said: "Lord, <u>You are God</u>, who made heaven and earth and the sea, and all that is in them. . .."*

God is the creator and sustainer of all things. He was at the beginning before there was a beginning. This is communicated in the very first words of the Bible:

Genesis 1:1 *In the beginning, God created the heavens and the earth.*

This is what God says about Himself:

Isaiah 55:8 *"For My thoughts are not your thoughts, Nor are your ways My ways," says the Lord.*

How different are God's ways and His thoughts from our ways and thoughts?

Isaiah 55:9 *"For as the heavens are higher than the earth, So are My ways higher than your ways, And My thoughts than your thoughts."*

When it comes to God, my dear one, we cannot assign our ways to Him. In a sense, it would be the same as a caterpillar trying to compare your ways to his ways.

God

You have immeasurably more abilities, strength, power, intelligence, thought processes, etc., when compared to a caterpillar. Even so, the deficit that exists between our ways and thoughts and God's ways and thoughts is infinitely more vast.

We cannot use our rational minds to comprehend God's wisdom. So what do we do? The Bible teaches us a very important way to look toward God. There are several key verses of scripture that will allow you to have a clearer understanding of a right relationship with God. The first one is this:

Psalms 14:1 *The fool has said in his heart, "There is no God."*

It is the foolish person who believes that there is no God. She has decided in her heart that He does not exist. To emphasize this point, the Bible repeats the exact same words in

The Prodigal Parent

Psalm 53:1 *The fool has said in his heart, "There is no God."* ...

I have often said that to believe the complex creation we live in "just happened" or that to suppose the earth naturally evolved to the point that it has without a supreme creator can be compared to finding a complicated Swiss watch in the woods—with all its intricate mechanisms and precision time-keeping abilities—and saying the watch just evolved to that state. You would think, "Now that's just ridiculous!" I ask you, how much more ridiculous is it to think that the sun was set at precisely the distance it needed to be from the earth to keep us warm but not burn us to death? Or that the earth is formed in such a way to not only sustain life but allow life to thrive? No, dear one, to think that creation just happened without THE CREATOR is indeed foolishness.

God

What I Should Have Taught You

Please do not be foolish. Resolve in your heart that God exists. Not only that, this next Scripture goes hand in hand:

> **Proverbs 1:7** *The fear of the LORD is the beginning of knowledge, But fools despise wisdom and instruction.*

Precious one, seek God, and ask Him to increase your faith, because this fact is true…

> **Hebrews 11:6** *But without faith it is impossible to please Him, for he who comes to God must believe that He is, and that He is a rewarder of those who diligently seek Him.*

You may say, "Well, I believe in God, but how do I have a relationship with God?"

The answer is to draw near to God. You must come to Him, and you must seek Him. You have to turn your heart toward Him.

> **Mark 12:33** *"And to love Him with all the heart, with all the understanding, with all the soul, and with all the strength. . .."*

My love, God longs to have you want Him and acknowledge your need for Him. In fact, He longs to bring you into a life-fulfilling relationship with Him.

> **Jeremiah 29:11-13** *For I know the thoughts that I think toward you, says the Lord, thoughts of peace and not of evil, to give you a future and a hope. Then you will call upon Me and go and*

pray to Me, and I will listen to you. And you will seek Me and find Me, when you search for Me with all your heart.

I have prayed for you often, and my prayer is always that God will watch over you and that you will know Him. Knowing God is having a relationship with God as Our Father. . .who is in heaven.

Finally, you must realize that:

John 4:24 *"God is Spirit, and those who worship Him must worship in spirit and truth."*

The Bible declares that God is Spirit, that He is not limited to the body. He is not limited to shape; He is not limited to boundaries or bonds; He is absolutely immeasurable and indiscernible to eyes that are limited to physical things. The

Bible declares that because God has no limitations, He can be everywhere at the same time.

God is a Spirit—infinite, eternal, and unchangeable.

These three words beautifully describe God. He is **infinite**: He is not body-bound. He is **eternal**: He has no beginning and no ending; He is forever self-existent. He is **unchangeable**: He never changes; the Bible declares that there is no variableness or shadow of turning with Him, which means He is forever faithful. Trust me when I tell you—you can trust Him!

My Prayer For You

My God and my Father, I ask that You help my precious loved one to seek You and to know You. I ask that any and all hindrances that block a true and fulfilling relationship with You, Father, be removed. I pray that You will help, guide, and lead my beloved to embrace You, to cherish You, and to know You. I ask that You provide what she needs in order to know that seeking You and Your kingdom is the most important thing that she can do for herself. I pray that You open the eyes of her understanding and that a deep longing to know You as her God and her Father overwhelm her. Father, I ask all this in the name of Jesus. Amen.

Jesus

God has revealed Himself to us through His son, Jesus Christ.

Everything I could hope to communicate to you about the Gospel (Good News) of Jesus Christ can be taken from the very first words in the Bible: "In the beginning God"! The first thing the Bible teaches us is that God is and that He began the beginning. Nothing begins without His foreknowledge:

> **Genesis 1:1** *In the beginning God created the heavens and the earth.*

Jesus

In the New Testament, the Book of John details the specifics regarding the completeness of His created effort:

> **John 1:3** *All things were made through Him, and without Him nothing was made that was made.*

Who is the Him? The Him is Jesus. The Him is the Word.

> **John 1:1** *In the beginning was the Word, and the Word was with God, and the Word was God.*

The Bible communicates that the Word was at the beginning, was with God, and was revealed to be God.

Later in the first chapter of the Book of John, the Bible definitively declares who the Word is:

John 1:14 *And <u>the Word became flesh and dwelt among us</u>, and we beheld His glory, the glory as of the <u>only begotten of the Father</u>, full of grace and truth.*

The above Scripture points to Jesus being God! ("...the Word was God"; "the Word became flesh and dwelt among us...") Jesus is God who dwelt among us! Jesus is the only begotten of the Father. My precious one, it so important that you understand that Jesus is the way to the Father:

John 1:18 *No one has seen God at any time. The only begotten Son, who is in the bosom of the Father, He has declared Him.*

Colossians 1:15 *He is the image of the invisible God, the firstborn over all creation.*

Jesus

1 John 4:2-3 *By this you know the Spirit of God: Every spirit that confesses that Jesus Christ has come in the flesh is of God, and every spirit that does not confess that Jesus Christ has come in the flesh is not of God.*

John 14:6 *Jesus said to him, "I am the way, the truth, and the life. No one comes to the Father except through Me."*

This is the key to exposing the misunderstanding that there are many religions and therefore many ways to God. Let us eliminate any confusion you may have. Although there are many religions, there is only one way to the truth and one way to God the Father. The above Scripture bears repeating:

John 14:6 *Jesus said to him, "I am the way, the truth, and the life. No one comes to the Father except through Me."*

What I Should Have Taught You

Jesus was sent to the world to be the sacrifice for our sins. This is so important to understand, my dear one. The only people who will accept that sacrifice are those who are drawn to the Lord, and the first step is to understand that we are all sinners in need of a savior. Sin is missing the mark and falling short of the standards God has set. When we realize in our hearts that we have fallen short of God's holiness and that we live sinful lives, then we cry out for Him to save us. When our hearts suffer and the reality of our sin becomes serious to us, that is when God's mercy and grace go to work. It is God who makes our hearts

Jesus

sensitive and registers to our innermost being that we are woefully lost without His mercy. That understanding, which comes to us by a spiritual tugging on our hearts, leads us to cry out to God for salvation.

God has made a way for us through the cross. Jesus died on that cross that we may have life; He died that we may live. God acknowledged the sacrifice of our Savior by raising Jesus from the dead. Jesus, who knew no sin because He never sinned, did not deserve to die. He was the perfect sacrifice for our sins:

> **2 Corinthians 5:21** *For He made Him who knew no sin to be sin for us, that we might become the righteousness of God in Him.*

> **John 3:16** *For God so loved the world that He gave His only begotten Son, that whoever*

*believes in Him should not perish
but have everlasting life.*

In the introduction to this book, I included Scripture that communicates the cost and the price that was paid for our salvation from chapter 53 of Isaiah. Centuries before Jesus walked the earth and centuries before John 3:16 was written, the words of the prophet Isaiah were penned:

> *But He was wounded for our transgressions,*
> *He was bruised for our iniquities;*
> *The chastisement for our peace was upon Him,*
> *And by His stripes we are healed.*
> *All we like sheep have gone astray;*
> *We have turned, every one, to his own way;*
> *And the Lord has laid on Him the iniquity of us all.*

Jesus

When you read these verses, it is clear that the Scripture speaks of Jesus and what will happen at the cross.

When the word of God begins to work on your heart, do not resist the calling of God. He wants to give you an abundant life. He wants to work through you to make you the best person you can be. When we surrender our lives to God through trusting in Jesus, God empowers our lives and begins to fulfill His will in our lives.

> **Revelation 3:20** *Behold, I stand at the door and knock. If anyone hears My voice and opens the door, I will come in to him and dine with him, and he with Me.*

The Prodigal Parent

My Prayer For You

Jesus, I pray that You will open the eyes of my precious one's understanding and that You will allow her to hear the knocking on the door to her heart. When she hears it, please help her to rush to that door and open it wide to You. Jesus, You promised that when that door is opened, You will come in and dine with her. I pray that You will allow my loved one to have the privilege of dining with You always, that she will know You and the power of Your might and the fellowship of Your suffering, and that her heart will be caught up in Your sacrifice for our sins. I pray, Lord, that all hindrances to her opening that door will be removed and all obstacles will be cleared out of the way. I thank You, Jesus, for Your great and precious promises and for Your ability and willingness to hear and answer our prayers. It is in Your mighty and majestic name that I pray. Amen.

Holy Spirit

The Holy Spirit is the third person of the Trinity: God the Father, God the Son, God the Holy Spirit. God is three persons in one. The Father sent the Son, and the Son has sent the Holy Spirit.

Jesus promised He would send the Holy Spirit:

> **John 15:26** *"But when the Helper comes, whom I shall send to you from the Father, the Spirit of truth who proceeds from the Father, He will testify of Me."*

The Father sent Jesus, and Jesus revealed the goodness and the love of God the Father to us. Likewise, Jesus sent the Holy Spirit; one of the Spirit's many roles is to testify and point us to Jesus.

> **John 16:13** *"However, when He, the Spirit of truth, has come, He will guide you into all truth; for He will not speak on His own authority, but whatever He hears He will speak; and He will tell you things to come."*

> **John 16:14** *"He will glorify Me, for He will take of what is Mine and declare it to you."*

> **John 14:17** *"...the Spirit of truth, whom the world cannot receive, because it neither sees Him nor knows Him; but you know Him,*

Holy Spirit

for He dwells with you and will be in you."

All the words above were spoken by Jesus. He was speaking to those who had made up their minds to follow Him. Jesus knew their lives would be full of trials and tribulations. He also knew we would need help today to live the purposeful lives He planned for us. This is where God the Holy Spirit comes in; He is the Helper:

John 14:16 *"And I will pray the Father, and He will give you another Helper, that He may abide with you forever—"*

God the Holy Spirit is the Helper that Jesus said He would send, and, in fact, has sent. All true believers have God the Holy Spirit living in them. This occurs during the moment of being "born again."

The Prodigal Parent

John 3:3 *Jesus answered and said to him, "Most assuredly, I say to you, unless one is born again, he cannot see the kingdom of God."*

John 3:5-6 *Jesus answered, "Most assuredly, I say to you, unless one is born of water and the Spirit, he cannot enter the kingdom of God. That which is born of the flesh is flesh, and that which is born of the Spirit is spirit."*

The Holy Spirit is present with all believers; He is God living within man. Now I know, dear one, that you may have some difficulty understanding this. However, please trust that I have prayed and asked God to open the eyes of your understanding that you may know the wonderful gift of God dwelling within you. That you may give your life to Jesus

Holy Spirit

Christ and be filled by the Holy Spirit is my constant plea to God the Father. When you have been born again, God the Holy Spirit takes up residency within you, for the Bible teaches:

> **1 Corinthians 6:19** *Or do you not know that your body is the temple of the Holy Spirit who is in you, whom you have from God, and you are not your own?*

In fact, without the Holy Spirit within, a person cannot belong to God:

> **Romans 8:9** *But you are not in the flesh but in the Spirit, if indeed the Spirit of God dwells in you. Now if anyone does not have the Spirit of Christ, he is not His.*

The Prodigal Parent

You see, my beloved, this is The Truth that I want you to see, even though it is a mystery:

> **Colossians 1:26** . . .*the mystery which has been hidden from ages and from generations, but now has been revealed to His saints.*

BUT NOW HAS BEEN REVEALED— Oh, my dear one, I so need you to see and know and embrace this! I long desperately for it to change your life and take you to a place from which you will never depart. I pray that God will manifest Himself to you through these writings in such a way that your life will be forever changed.

What exactly is this mystery that I want God to reveal to you?

> **Colossians 1:27** *To them God willed to make known what are the*

riches of the glory of this mystery among the Gentiles: which is Christ in you, the hope of glory.

Yes, Christ in you—there it is—through His Spirit, God living in you! Know that your body is the temple of the Holy Spirit. Oh, my beloved, I speak as if it is the case even now because I trust and believe my God will make it so. I plead with the Father of all creation to move upon you through His Spirit. It was God the Holy Spirit who moved upon the earth in the act of creation:

> **Genesis 1:2** *The earth was without form, and void; and darkness was on the face of the deep. And the Spirit of God was hovering over the face of the waters.*

I pray the Holy Spirit will hover over you and make you all that you are meant

The Prodigal Parent

to be in God. I know He can; I believe He will. However, you must be born again. You must profess with your mouth the Lord Jesus and believe in your heart that God raised him from the dead. Yes, God raised Him from the dead, and He did this by the power of His Spirit:

> **Romans 8:11** *But if the Spirit of Him who raised Jesus from the dead dwells in you, He who raised Christ from the dead will also give life to your mortal bodies through His Spirit who dwells in you.*

You see, my precious one, the same Spirit of God who worked at the beginning in creation is the Spirit of Him who raised Jesus from the dead—and is the Spirit indwelling all born-again believers.

Holy Spirit

The reality of the presence of the Holy Spirit within the believer comes from hearing the word of God and trusting in its truth. This simply means believing the good news that salvation has come through Jesus and that your sins can be forgiven if you put your trust in Jesus.

> **Ephesians 1:13-14** *In Him you also trusted, after you heard the word of truth, the gospel of your salvation; in whom also, having believed, you were sealed with the Holy Spirit of promise, who is the guarantee of our inheritance until the redemption of the purchased possession, to the praise of His glory.*

The Prodigal Parent

What I Should Have Taught You

God the Holy Spirit is the third person of the Trinity: God the Father, God the Son, and God the Holy Spirit. God is three parts in one, just like you consist of body, soul, and spirit. Our connection with God in a knowing sense is through and by His Holy Spirit. Jesus promised to ask the Father to send Him. Jesus said He would not leave us or abandon us, that we who believe will know His very presence and that we will be assured that He is with us always—even until the end of the world. When you are born again, you are adopted into the family of God. You are so precious to me, but to be a child of God is much more precious. I love you so much, but my love cannot compare to how much God loves you and wants you to be His child.

Holy Spirit

My Prayer For You

My God and my Father, I ask that You hear this prayer and move upon the heart of my precious one. I pray that You will speak to her and that Your Holy Spirit will fill her. I ask that You pour out Your grace upon her that she may know You and the power of Your might. I pray that she will receive and know the blessed assurance of Your Spirit within her. Oh Lord, please show Your mercy and love to her. May Your Spirit forever dwell in her! I ask this in the name of Your Son and our savior, Jesus the Christ. Amen.

The Bible

I can honestly tell you that I read the Bible almost daily. When I don't take the time to read, I almost always wish I had. It is without a doubt the greatest book ever written. Its pages contain all that you need to navigate this world and experience all that God has planned for you. It is the best and only real food for your soul. Just like your favorite meal, it becomes something for which you truly long. The Bible provides more than you can digest with regard to knowledge and insight. The wisdom found within its passages is beyond complete comprehension.

The Bible

I ask you to reflect on these words spoken by Jesus when He was tempted by the devil:

Matthew 4:4 *But He answered and said, "It is written, 'Man shall not live by bread alone, but by every word that proceeds from the mouth of God.'"*

Jesus' words are a direct insight into the richness and power that exist in being filled with the Word of God, the Bible! It is joy in the midst of sadness; it is peace in the midst of any storm; it is wisdom when you are not sure what to do; it is light when you find yourself in the dark; it is hope when you feel hopeless; it is help when you feel helpless; it is comfort when you face uncomfortable times. The Bible is a compass when you have lost your direction. When you feel at your wits' end, it will show you a new beginning. In other

The Prodigal Parent

words, it will be as described in the Book of Psalms:

> **Psalm 119:105** *Your word is a lamp to my feet And a light to my path.*

I pray that God will guide you to and through the pages of the Bible. I pray that you will find joy and delight in devouring the manna of the Word of God. I pray that you will fall in love with reading and studying the Bible.

Someone created a great acronym for the letters B I B L E:

Basic **I**nstructions **B**efore **L**eaving **E**arth

This is a fitting description because it indicates where to find all you need to know about God, Jesus, and the Holy Spirit. The Bible provides the pathway to establishing

The Bible

a rich and rewarding relationship between you and the Creator.

Yes, dear one, all this and more is found in the pages of the Bible. All the wisdom that you need to navigate the journey of life is contained in the Bible. As I mentioned above, I pray that God will grant you the desire to devour His Word. The need to study the Bible is a powerful habit. This habit will lead you in the right direction and bring you success in life:

> **Joshua 1:8** *"This Book of the Law shall not depart from your mouth, but you shall meditate in it day and night, that you may observe to do according to all that is written in it. For then you will make your way prosperous, and then you will have good success."*

The Prodigal Parent

I do not hesitate to repeat my prayer for you to be driven to God's Word and become a faithful student of the Bible — what a wonderful habit to possess!

My desire is that you immediately begin to read the Bible every day. Yes, every day! You may read a little; you may read a lot. However, this I can assure you: once you commit to read His Word daily, God will reveal to you the wondrous and glorious truths in His Word. Not only that, He will begin to reveal Himself to you in such a way that you will develop an intimate relationship with Him. When you seek Him in His Word, you will find Him. You will find Him present to help in your time of need. You will find He is a friend who sticks closer than a brother. The time you spend in His Word will never be wasted. You will grow in knowledge and find out more about yourself than you can even imagine.

The Bible

What I Should Have Taught You

The Bible contains the wisdom needed to live life. It provides a road map that will help you in every part of your life. God gave His Word to us that we might know our purpose and position with regard to Him and to others. The pages of the Bible are filled with truth, and if you know it:

> **John 8:32** *"And you shall know the truth, and the truth shall make you free."*

The person who looks into the truth of God's Word will find knowledge and blessings more abundant than can be imagined. Study the Bible and see what God will do with you, for you, and through you!

The Bible is God's gift to humankind. However, as with any gift, unless you open it, you will not discover the treasure inside.

The Prodigal Parent

I implore you to run to the treasure and wisdom of the Bible. Allow the richness of its insights to wash over you. I encourage you to search the stories and learn the lessons taught within its pages.

> **Psalm 34:8** *Oh, taste and see that the Lord is good; Blessed is the man who trusts in Him!*

My Prayer For You

Lord, I pray that my precious one will have the desire to read and study Your Word—that it will become a regular part of her day and become just as essential as eating every day. I pray that her desire will grow strong and her need to meet You in the pages of the Bible will become the most important part of her daily life. I ask You to open Your Word to her and cause a hunger that will only be sated by tasting the sweetness of the wisdom, knowledge,

The Bible

and comfort that comes from spending time with You, my God and Father, in Your Bible. I ask this in the matchless name of my Lord and Savior, Jesus. Amen.

Faith

Precious one, faith is absolutely necessary for a relationship with God. It is the mechanism by which we know that God IS—meaning that He is God, the Creator of the heavens, the earth, the sea, and everything that is in them. How can you know God exists if you have never seen God? The answer is through faith!

> **Hebrews 11:1** *Now faith is the substance of things hoped for, the evidence of things not seen.*

> **Hebrews 11:6** *But without faith it is impossible to please Him, for he who comes to God must believe that He is, and that*

Faith

> *He is a rewarder of those who diligently seek Him.*

Therein lie both the problem and the solution. As the Scripture states, there must be belief that He is—that God IS. This means there must be an acknowledgement that God is real. This is the first and foremost challenge, and it is answered with this awareness: by faith we understand.

> **Psalm 14:1** *The fool has said in his heart, "There is no God."*

Yes, the Bible calls the person who does not believe in the existence of God a fool. Not only that, the foolish man thinks matters regarding the Spirit of God are foolishness:

> **1 Corinthians 2:14** *But the natural man does not receive the things of the Spirit of God, for*

they are foolishness to him; nor can he know them, because they are spiritually discerned.

Read what God says in the Bible about Himself:

Isaiah 45:18 *For thus says the Lord, Who created the heavens, Who is God, Who formed the earth and made it, Who has established it, Who did not create it in vain, Who formed it to be inhabited:* ***"I am the Lord, and there is no other."***

So how does a person move from fool to faith and from foolishness to faithfulness?

Romans 10:17 *So then faith comes by hearing, and hearing by the word of God.*

Faith

You see, dear one, it is God who decided how faith—that is, saving faith, real faith, life-changing faith—would come to humankind. He created humankind with intellect and the ability to reason. The Bible tells us:

> **Isaiah 1:18** *"Come now, and let us reason together," Says the Lord, "Though your sins are like scarlet, They shall be as white as snow; Though they are red like crimson, They shall be as wool."*

About what exactly is God calling us to reason together with Him?

Simply put, He is stating that you must rely on someone other than yourself to be saved—and that you do need to be saved.

God knows we are sinners. God also knows that we know we are sinners, and we know that He knows we know this. It is no secret. Inside of each person is a fallen, sinful nature. No matter how we try to deny, hide, or reason it away, we know this to be true.

This reasoning that God asks of us is not a complicated thought process, and that is why little children are able to ask Jesus to save them. God created us with the ability to realize our need for Him. However, our human thoughts lean toward rebellion. We desire to be self-governing. We are disobedient when we refuse to submit to the tugging in our hearts toward God. The desire to be self-governing pulls powerfully toward destruction. Disobedience drives our sinful nature and places us at odds with God.

However, God provided a path for our redemption by sending His only Son Jesus as atonement for our sins. Jesus is the sacrifice who paid the price of our sins for

Faith

us. Without faith, we would not be able to comprehend God's great gift to us through Jesus. Without faith, we would not understand what Jesus did. It is only through God's grace that we know to reach out and call on Him for salvation.

> **Ephesians 2:8** *For by grace you have been saved through faith, and that not of yourselves; it is the gift of God....*

The Lord utilized reasoning to reach people:

> **Romans 10:14** *How then shall they call on Him in whom they have not believed? And how shall they believe in Him of whom they have not heard? And how shall they hear without a preacher?*

The Prodigal Parent

Unfortunately, people—and I hope you really get this—believe themselves to be wise but do not understand that their wisdom is not on any level near the wisdom of God. That is why the Bible warns humanity this way:

> **1 Corinthians 1:18** *For the message of the cross is foolishness to those who are perishing, but to us who are being saved it is the power of God.*

> **1 Corinthians 1:21** *For since, in the wisdom of God, the world through wisdom did not know God, it pleased God through the foolishness of the message preached to save those who believe.*

Therefore, my dear one, as the Apostle Paul writes, life is lived by faith:

Faith

Romans 1:16-17 *For I am not ashamed of the gospel of Christ, for it is the power of God to salvation for everyone who believes, for the Jew first and also for the Greek. For in it the righteousness of God is revealed from faith to faith; as it is written, "The just shall live by faith."*

Faith that saves is having faith in the work of God in sending His Son to redeem us.

John 3:16 *For God so loved the world that He gave His only begotten Son, that whoever believes in Him should not perish but have everlasting life.*

Jesus said:

> **John 14:1** *"Let not your heart be troubled; you believe in God, believe also in Me."*

The Bible is clear, therefore allow me to be also. This is my motivation as I write to you:

> **John 20:31** *. . .but these are written that you may believe that Jesus is the Christ, the Son of God, and that believing you may have life in His name.*

What I Should Have Taught You

Faith is real, and faith in God is what is most important for you to understand. As I write to you, I am trusting God the Father through God the Holy Spirit to reveal to you by faith God the Son—Jesus. I am telling you this now and trusting that by faith you may believe, and by believing,

Faith

that you may have a more abundant life in Christ Jesus. I am trusting God and His Word that faith comes by hearing the Word of God, that as you read the Word you will receive, believe, and trust Christ as your savior.

My Prayer For You

Heavenly Father, You who have set all things in motion and know all things, I come to You asking and believing that You hear my prayer. Father, I know You and trust You in all things. I have seen my faith grow and expand in so many areas of my life. I recognize the precious faith You have provided to me and understand how You have cultivated it in such a way that I can come to You and ask for anything. Lord, I ask that You grant my child, whom I love, a life of faith. I pray for a strong life of faith, a saving life of faith,

The Prodigal Parent

and an abundant life of faith for her. I ask for her faith to grow strong; I ask for her to understand the power of that faith. Father, You said in Your Word that if we have mustard-seed size faith, we will move mountains. I pray Your hand of grace will guide my beloved to great faith, a faith that will work to please You. I pray that through that faith, she may walk in the newness of life and in the grace that only You can provide, Father. I also ask for her to have a rich, rewarding, Christ-centered life in daily fellowship with Your Holy Spirit. I ask all this in the matchless name of Jesus. Amen.

Prayer

My dear one, prayer is to God. He is the audience and the object of all prayers. Prayer is not like meditation, although prayer does have a direct effect on us and others. That's right—we should pray for ourselves, and we should pray for others. God will intervene for the benefit of others through and because of our prayers. The Bible teaches us that we can and should pray for others:

> **James 5:16** *Confess your trespasses to one another, and pray for one another, that you may be healed. The effective, fervent prayer of a righteous man avails much.*

I can honestly say that I have prayed for you more times than I can count. I have prayed that God will watch over you, protect you, bless you, and prosper you. Most of all, I have prayed that God will give you a heart that embraces His son Jesus as your Lord and Savior. I have prayed that your faith will grow, that you will be strengthened to your inner-most being by the very presence of the Holy Spirit, and that God might use you for His purpose. I believe God has heard my prayers. I continue to pray for you to this day.

True prayer is us going to God. We come to Him, believing He is able to do anything, asking Him for the help we need, knowing He is God, and needing Him—His wisdom, His guidance, His forgiveness, His mercy, and His grace.

Hebrews 4:16 *Let us therefore come boldly to the throne of grace,*

Prayer

that we may obtain mercy and find grace to help in time of need.

I need God's help in many ways. One of the most pressing ways is in reaching out to you to let you know just how much I love you and God loves you. I will always continue to pray for you.

Prayer is done on earth but heard in heaven. We pray that God may be engaged by us. Jesus taught us this about prayer:

Matthew 6:6 *"But you, when you pray, go into your room, and when you have shut your door, pray to your Father who is in the secret place; and your Father who sees in secret will reward you openly."*

Jesus also said:

Matthew 7:7 *"Ask, and it will be given to you; seek, and you will find; knock, and it will be opened to you."*

Matthew 7:11 *"If you then, being evil, know how to give good gifts to your children, how much more will your Father who is in heaven give good things to those who ask Him!"*

You see, my dear one, Jesus made plain that God is not like humankind. He has not and cannot do evil. If we earthly parents—with all our faults, failures, and shortcomings—give gifts to our children, then God is surely willing and able to give good things to those who ask Him.

There is a stipulation though:

Prayer

James 1:6-7 *But let him ask in faith, with no doubting, for he who doubts is like a wave of the sea driven and tossed by the wind. For let not that man suppose that he will receive anything from the Lord. . ..*

We have to ask in faith. Yes, the faith we discussed in the previous chapter.

Hebrews 11:6 *But without faith it is impossible to please Him, for he who comes to God must believe that He is, and that He is a rewarder of those who diligently seek Him.*

The fact is that God wants His children (His children—those who belong to the family of God) to ask of Him in prayer. Our prayers demonstrate our trust and belief in Him. We are not wishing; we are asking

The Prodigal Parent

God our Father, who is able to do all things, to help us in any and all situations. Think about this: God gave His only begotten Son to die on the cross so that your sins and my sins would be forgiven. If He did that, tell me what He won't do for us!

> **Romans 8:32** *He who did not spare His own Son, but delivered Him up for us all, how shall He not with Him also freely give us all things?*

We make all sorts of prayers to God—for all things, in all situations, under all circumstances. There is no limit on our ability to ask God and seek God. In fact, we are encouraged to seek Him this way:

> **Jeremiah 33:3** *"'Call to Me, and I will answer you, and show you great and mighty things, which you do not know.'"*

Prayer

God established this form of communication and has demonstrated His willingness to hear us through our prayers. Prayer is a person speaking to God and God responding to her through His divine actions.

Psalm 143:1 *Hear my prayer, O Lord, Give ear to my supplications! In Your faithfulness answer me, And in Your righteousness.*

There is no established pattern or methodology to how we pray. Our main task is to come with belief and trust in God, for the Bible teaches that we often do not know what to pray or how to pray:

Romans 8:26 *Likewise the Spirit also helps in our weaknesses. For we do not know what we should pray for as we ought, but the Spirit Himself makes intercession* *for us with groanings which cannot be uttered.*

Prayer is honest. Children pray because they believe God hears their prayers, and that is strong proof for how prayer works. Prayer is being honest with God and letting Him know that we are coming to Him because He is the sustainer and supplier of our needs. Prayer is a demonstration of our need for Him and our belief that He hears and can answer our prayers. In coming to God, we recognize our limitations and acknowledge His unlimited power. We seek God's presence and power in our lives when we pray. We understand that He has the ultimate say in who we are, what we are, and where we are. Prayer is both asking God and telling God: asking for His help with our needs and telling Him we know that we need Him. When we pray, we let God know that we are lost without His help. This is why prayer should be constant.

Prayer

1 Thessalonians 5:17 *...pray without ceasing...*

Philippians 4:6 *Be anxious for nothing, but in everything by prayer and supplication, with thanksgiving, let your requests be made known to God....*

I leave this last point about prayer with you:

Luke 11:1 *Now it came to pass, as He was praying in a certain place, when He ceased, that one of His disciples said to Him, "Lord, teach us to pray, as John also taught his disciples."*

The profoundness of this Scripture really gets to me. Jesus was praying to God the Father, His disciples were observing Him, and a disciple asked, "Teach us to

The Prodigal Parent

pray." This is so profound to me because it demonstrates that a person must have the desire to pray. That is the essential foundation: you must want to pray. Without this desire you will never do it. If you have the desire, even though you feel inadequate, weak, or feeble, you can do exactly what that disciple did. If you think you do not know how, you can ask, "Lord, teach me to pray." God will answer your prayer just as Jesus did for His disciple in Luke's account of Jesus' ministry:

> So He said to them, "When you pray, say:
> Our Father in heaven,
> Hallowed be Your name.
> Your kingdom come.
> Your will be done
> On earth as it is in heaven.
> Give us day by day our daily bread.
> And forgive us our sins,

For we also forgive everyone
who is indebted to us.
And do not lead us into temptation,
But deliver us from the evil one."

What I Should Have Taught You

I believe God hears and answers prayers. I believe that when we let others know we have prayed for them, it is similar to letting them know we have made a deposit into their bank accounts. The deposit is there, and the recipients do not need receipts. I have prayed for you, and as long as I have breath, I will be praying for you. The person who prays demonstrates her understanding and need for God's power in her life. When we pray, we show our faith in God and our belief that He is ever-present, ever-willing, and ever-able. Remember above all that God is able to do exceedingly and abundantly more than we could ever ask or imagine. He is a very present help in time of need. You can trust me when I tell you that prayer works.

My Prayer For You

My God and my Father, I pray You will continue to watch over my beloved one and that You will protect and bless this precious one of mine. You have honored my life with her love, and I come now, as I have so many times before, asking for Your hand on her life. Bless the prayer life of my child. Bless her, that she may pray and find true fellowship with You, Father. Guide her to Your throne of grace to find mercy and grace to help in time of need. Create the way for my precious one to have a faithful and rewarding prayer life. I ask this in the name of Your Son and our Savior, Jesus Christ our Lord! Amen.

Salvation

Ephesians 2:8 *For by grace you have been saved through faith, and that not of yourselves; it is the gift of God....*

My precious one, please hear me and focus on what I am about to say:

Salvation comes by grace through Jesus Christ. It is the gift of God, and it is received through faith in the Son of God and His sacrifice on the cross. Salvation is the process of the miraculous transforming power of God through the gospel of Jesus Christ:

Romans 1:16 *For I am not ashamed of the gospel of Christ, for it is the power of God to salvation for everyone who believes. . ..*

If what you are reading is penetrating and stirring you, please understand that the gift of God is near you, working in and upon you. It is grace: God's unmerited favor. We don't deserve it, and we can't earn it. If you are moved to put your trust in God, that is the grace of God at work!

Grace reaches out for you and draws you to Him. How wonderful that draw is, how very precious it is to be sought after by God. Many people say, "I found God." Let me tell you, dear one, that is not how it works. God was never, ever lost! We are the lost ones, and God finds us. He seeks us out; He draws us to Him. It is His loving kindness, which is better than life itself,

Salvation

that reaches for us and draws us to Him. He is the one who establishes our relationship with Him. God reveals Himself to us, and the Bible says we love Him for a reason:

1 John 4:19 *We love Him because He first loved us.*

You see, our relationship with God is established by Him. We come to Him because His love reaches out for us. As you are reading these words and your heart opens to receive them, please know that it is God reaching for you, drawing you, and calling to you. He is the one who settles our wandering hearts to land in His gracious, loving, and outstretched arms!

By grace we are saved. The gospel of Christ is the power that draws us to the salvation that God has prepared for all who believe. Listen to my words and allow them to ring in your heart and mind.

The Prodigal Parent

We are all sinners. I have sinned, and you have sinned—all humankind has sinned. Our sin separates us from God; in fact, the penalty for sin is death!

Romans 6:23 *For the wages of sin is death, but the gift of God is eternal life in Christ Jesus our Lord.*

The above Scripture highlights both the negative "death," which is earned from the "wages of sin," and the positive "eternal life," which is given by God through Christ Jesus. The death spoken of here is eternal death—being eternally separated from a loving and caring God. This is the final state for all who are not saved. It does not mean physical death because everyone will die physically. No, dear one, we are speaking of what happens after that. Where will a person spend eternity? The death spoken of here is the death that

Salvation

places a person forever away from God. If that sounds like hell, that's because it is.

This awareness about death is so important and essential for you to understand, my precious one. Surely we need the help of the Lord to show the way!

What would your answer be if I asked you, "Are you a sinner?" If you are honest, there is only one answer to that question: "Yes, I am a sinner. I have sinned, and I do sin." Now, that affirmative answer would be the absolute truth (whether we admit it or not). The Bible is clear:

> **Romans 3:23** . . *for all have sinned and fall short of the glory of God*. . .

There are no sinless people. We have all done things and do things that have earned us the label "sinner." Therefore, when we combine our understanding that we are all sinners to our knowledge about the wages of sin, we see that what people should earn for their sins is eternal death.

Of course, you might ask yourself, "Why would God allow all who sinned to die if we are all sinners?" The answer is that God does not want us to pay the price of eternal death for our sins. A very familiar Scripture comes into play here:

> **John 3:16** *"For God so loved the world that He gave His only begotten Son, that whoever believes in Him should not perish but have everlasting life."*

Now the very next verse helps our understanding by making Jesus' point even clearer:

Salvation

John 3:17 *"For God did not send His Son into the world to condemn the world, but that the world through Him might be saved."*

God the Creator and Sustainer of all things made a way for humankind to be saved from sin. The eternal death we earned through our sins was paid for by the sinless Savior Jesus Christ. The fact is that God provided a sacrifice to deliver us from the punishment of eternal death, which is condemnation and eternal separation from God. God does not want you eternally outside His kingdom and forever separated from His love and mercy.

Those who are not saved will never enter the kingdom of God:

John 3:3 *Jesus answered and said to him, "Most assuredly, I say to* *you, unless one is born again, he cannot see the kingdom of God."*

According to Jesus, those who realize they are sinners, repent their sins, and receive Him as Savior and Lord are born again—not physically, but spiritually!

Hear me, my dearest one. I am fully trusting God at this moment to help me present this to you. I know that God wants you to understand and fully embrace His love for you! I am, at this very moment, trusting the Lord to present Himself to you so that you will know what it means to be born again!

The truth is that humankind is dead in its sins. This death is a separation from God. People are in rebellion against God, His authority, and His rightful place as God the Creator. Humankind refuses to accept that it is subject to God and has an absolute need for God! It is a fact that before being born again, a person does not really want to believe in God. Oh, we may say, "I believe in God," but we look to ourselves as the center of the world and reject the thought that God is truly the Giver and Sustainer of all life. We do not want to accept that He is Ruler of all, He is greater than all, and He sits higher than all. More specifically, we despise the fact that we are subject to Him and accountable to Him! We hide our eyes from the truth, mainly because if we deny the truth then we somehow believe it is less than the truth. That, my dear, is not the case! All creation is subject to Him, and we are without excuse!

The Bible states:

> **Romans 1:20-21** *For since the creation of the world His invisible attributes are clearly seen, being understood by the*

things that are made, even His eternal power and Godhead, so that they are without excuse, because, although they knew God, they did not glorify Him as God, nor were thankful, but became futile in their thoughts, and their foolish hearts were darkened.

There it is, precious one—there is the issue: humankind rebelliously and foolishly refuses to acknowledge the truth, even though deep inside we know that there is a God! The wedge that pushes us away is knowing that if we acknowledge Him and His rightful place in our lives as the Creator, we are merely His creatures—it means we are subject to Him. This truth does not align with our will and desire to run things our own way. Simply put, God gets in the way of how we want to live.

Salvation

"If I don't think about Him and acknowledge Him the way I know I should, and if I choose to bear little or no allegiance to Him, then I can live the way I want." These are the basic thoughts of all humans. If not for God's love pursuing us, in spite of our rebellion, we would all be eternally lost and condemned to hell. However, God's love for us is so great that He pursues us with an everlasting love. In spite of our rejection, He pursues; in spite of our wandering, He pursues; in spite of our sin, He pursues!

Listen to what the Bible says regarding the love of God:

> **Romans 5:8** *But God demonstrates His own love toward us, in that while we were still sinners, Christ died for us.*

Listen to how The Message Bible makes it plain and direct:

The Prodigal Parent

Colossians 1:21-22 *You yourselves are a case study of what he does. At one time you all had your backs turned to God, thinking rebellious thoughts of him, giving him* [sic] *trouble every chance you got. But now, by giving himself completely at the Cross, actually dying for you, Christ brought you over to God's side and put your lives together, whole and holy in his presence.*

How do you turn your back on a gift like that? You don't. You can't. I pray you won't!

What I Should Have Taught You

I want you to know that you are so very precious to me and that I love you with such a deep love that at times it is difficult to express. However, no matter how much I

Salvation

love you, God loves you more. He has provided for you, through His grace, salvation for your soul! You see, my dear one, sin separates us from God. We are all sinners, and without a way to salvation, we would all be lost. Praise God, for He has made salvation possible through His Son Jesus Christ. Christ died on the cross and paid the price for our sins—your sins and my sins. With His death, He paid for our salvation. Yes, that means He died so that you might have eternal life. He was the only substitute who could have paid this price for us. He who knew no sin became sin for us that we might gain eternal life.

This salvation is a gift from God, but like any gift, it must be received. You may ask, "But how do I receive this gift?" The answer is through faith. The truth is that no one gets saved until she admits she is lost. The truth is that a person must believe God exists and that He is the Creator and

The Prodigal Parent

Sustainer of all. Finally, a person must first admit she is a sinner in need of a savior and that God is the only hope. In that moment, faith enters, takes over, and allows her to step out of darkness and into His marvelous light.

Remember, God is never lost—we are lost, and God draws us to Him. There are times and events in your life God uses to draw you to Him. He is reaching out for you, and you will know Him when you find yourself caught up in the wondrous, loving arms of God the Father through faith in His Son Jesus. The Bible teaches that if you confess the Lord Jesus with your mouth and believe in your heart that God raised Him from the dead, you will be saved. With the heart, one believes unto righteousness; with the mouth, confession is made unto salvation.

Salvation

My Prayer For You

My God and my Father, I come to You asking that You open the eyes of understanding and grant to my beloved the gift of salvation. I pray that any and all hindrances be removed, that Your loving arms open to her, and that she rushes into them. I pray that You will not cease to draw her to You until she arrives safely into Your very presence. Increase her faith, open closed doors, and light the way that she may be saved through Your mercy and by Your grace. In Jesus' name, I pray. Amen.

The Church

I have been asked this question many times:

"Do I have to go to church to be a Christian?"

I have always answered the same way:

"No, you do not have to go to church to be a Christian—but Christians go to church!"

They go because there is a desire to be with the people of God. They go because there is an inner desire to be in the midst of other believers and to have fellowship with them. Christians love to be with other

The Church

Christians. It is not a religious thing; it is a desire thing. It is actually no different than the desire to be with your friends or your crew or, for that matter, your family. Christians draw strength, encouragement, and insight from one another. They love being in the presence of each other. The Message Bible gives insight into why this is:

> **Proverbs 27:17** *You use steel to sharpen steel, and one friend sharpens another.*

Christians love to be in corporate worship with one another, and through the assembly, they find there is something apart from themselves that is fulfilled by being in a congregation of believers. I know today, in the midst of the information age where everything is available online, there is a tendency to say, "Why bother?" when you can just tune in, hear the sermon, and sing along with the praise and worship.

However, any real Christian will tell you there is nothing like being there. We can watch the game on TV, but nothing is like being court side. God established the church and knitted our hearts together in a way that our lives are truly enriched when we come together.

"Do I have to go to church to be a Christian?"

"No, but Christians desire to go to church!"

I am finishing this book during the COVID-19 pandemic. Some churches have been unable to meet in person for months, and many Sunday services have been moved online. I can honestly tell you that although the Word goes out from the same pulpit and the praying and the singing are the same, the missing element is the fellowship—being there together in the house of the Lord. King David speaks of the joy of going to the house of the Lord:

> **Psalm 122:1** *I was glad when they said to me, "Let us go into the house of the Lord."*

However, my dear, I want to draw your attention to some higher thoughts regarding the church—higher than the building where people assemble and much higher than what happens when we gather at a certain place on a certain day at a certain time. I want to focus your attention on two things from the Bible that Jesus made very clear. The first is this:

> **Matthew 16:18** *"And I also say to you that you are Peter, and on this rock **I will build My church**, and the gates of Hades shall not prevail against it."*

The Prodigal Parent

The first point is that the church was built by Jesus. I am not referring to a building or an address but the church as the institution created and constructed by the heavenly architect Jesus Himself. This means that the church exists for and because of Christ and Him alone. No human can take credit for building the church, and no building can stand alone as the church.

> **Isaiah 66:1** *Thus says the Lord: "Heaven is My throne, And earth is My footstool. Where is the house that you will build Me? And where is the place of My rest?"*

Oh yes, my dear, the church is much more than a building. It is the assembly of called-out believers who have been born again and await the return of the King of Kings and the Lord of Lords. It is the safe haven where we who believe are moored

The Church

and find peace for our storm-tossed souls. It is the place we run to in prayer and thanksgiving, knowing that we will be met by our Savior Jesus. He is able to do for us what we cannot do for ourselves.

The church is so much more than a building! It is the body of Christ here on earth. It is His arms that hug the lonely. It is His riches that feed the hungry and clothe the naked. It is His on-time Word that touches and restores our broken and bruised souls. It is His joy that provides strength to the weak. It is the key that unlocks the door to the captives. It is the song that lifts the fallen spirit. It is mercy in time of trouble. It is faith when all seems broken. When you just can't bear any more, it carries your heavy load. Oh, if my words could only touch you the way I feel them right now. I pray to God they can!

The Prodigal Parent

Jesus said, "I will build"! There is much to contemplate in those words, the first of which is that it will be done. You can be one hundred percent sure that the church exists by this one statement alone. Jesus did not leave it to humanity; He Himself said He will be the builder. This same Jesus who made all things—the heaven, the earth, and the sea—said "I will build." Therefore, all wonder and doubt as to the existence of the church should be put to rest. If He who created the ground you stand on and the air you breathe, the trees and the birds, you and I, and all that we see said "I will build," then you can trust it was built by Him. My dear one, let this thought penetrate your very being. If Jesus built it, don't you want to be a part of it? Think about that!!! Why would anyone decide to remain outside of the church? If Jesus built it, then I want to be a part of it!

The Church

The second thing I want to draw your attention to is this: Jesus said, "I will build My church." He was specific about to whom the church belonged: He said "My church." I want you to think about what He was saying here and, specifically, to what he was referring. The church is not a building; rather, it is a gathering of citizens called out—a Christian community of members on earth, saints in heaven, or both. Jesus set the foundation and dug it deep and wide. The church has been under construction since He started His ministry, and His work continues to this day. He adds to His church daily, and no one can measure the size of it. It is greater than any building humanity has created and more vast than our minds can conceive. It reaches to the highest mountain, and it flows to the lowest valley. Its walls are unscalable, and its rooms are too many to number. My dear child, please know that the church is real—so very real that Jesus did not trust people to build it. He Himself set out to build the church, and it is so much more than a building. Think about these words that Jesus spoke:

> **Matthew 18:20** *"For where two or three are gathered together in My name, I am there in the midst of them."*

Do you see any mention of a building? No. However, there is a clear indication of gathering together. There is a clear indication of the unity of assembly. This tells us that no Christian was meant to stand alone. The fact is, we need one another; we need the fellowship that comes from assembling together. When we come together, Jesus the builder of the church has said He will be there with us!

There is something—a part of the whole—missing due to the pandemic keeping us apart. The missing element of fellowship with each other is real. Yes, we talk on the phone, and we have Zoom meetings where we are able to see each other, but there is something missing in not being together in the sanctuary of God. Church is a part of a believer. Being in the house of the Lord with the saints of God; being in the fellowship of believers and sharing with one another; seeing, greeting, and lifting one another up in prayer and encouragement—this is real and meaningful, and it is missed during this time in our lives.

What I Should Have Taught You

The church was and is constructed by Jesus. He is the one who built His church. We are the ones who have the benefit and privilege of being a part of His church. He provided access to the church and calls all who believe to gather in His name to worship freely and receive of His goodness,

His mercy, and His eternal love. There are no walls that can contain His church, and in fact, where two or three are gathered in His name, He Himself, the builder, has promised to be there with that small gathering. Ah, but yet how great a gathering shall there be in the end when He gathers the whole church together! We see glimpses of that when we find ourselves assembled together on Sunday mornings or in mid-week services where the called-out believers come together for corporate praise and worship.

Do you have to go to church to be a Christian? No—but Christians go to church!

My Prayer For You

My God and Father in heaven, I pray You will impress upon the heart of my child the desire and longing to gather with

The Church

believers and unite with them in corporate praise and worship. I ask that You allow her to be able to say, just like King David said, *I was glad when they said to me, "Let us go into the house of the Lord."* I ask this in the name of Him who built and sustains the church. In Jesus' name I pray. Amen.

The Cross

John 12:32-33 *"And I, if I am lifted up from the earth, will draw all peoples to Myself." This He said, signifying by what death He would die.*

The cross is the place of sacrifice of our Lord and Savior, where God the Father placed the sins of the world on God the Son. My beloved, if there is one place that I would have taken you a long time ago, it would have been to the foot of the cross. That destination and the view from that particular vantage point are both breathtaking and awe-inspiring. Anyone who truly looks up from the foot of the cross will never be the same. The view from that position will alter the rest of a person's life. Now, I do not mean I would have taken you to a physical place; no, I would have sat you down and explained to you what happened at the cross and because of the cross.

There is a hymn that goes like this:

At the cross, at the cross,
Where I first saw the light,
And the burden of my heart rolled away;
It was there by faith I received my sight....

These words are so reflective of what happens when the reality of the cross of Christ penetrates a person's being. The reality of what took place on the old, rugged cross is uncovered when a person realizes that Jesus took upon Himself the sins of the world—your sins, my sins, and everyone else's sins. He became the sacrifice, the perfect sacrifice, and the only possible sacrifice that would save our souls.

The Prodigal Parent

My dear, it doesn't take a lot of effort to recognize just how wicked and sinful this world is. The news is filled with the acts of a heartless humankind and the lack of peace that accompanies the sins of humanity. There really is no need to convince you that the world is desperately wicked and that without a Savior, humankind is lost. I realize that, for the most part, we tend to rationalize these sins away. We seem to think the world will just keep on moving forward, and our lives will move forward with the world. However, I ask you to stop, think for a minute, and focus on this thought: What happens. . .when it's over? What does that mean to you? Obviously, this life will come to an end. Every day when we wake up, we should realize that somebody else did not. That's the point— someday it will be the last day, for all of us. Then what happens?

The Cross

If we stand at the foot of the cross, we can gain perspective regarding the ultimate outcome that each of us will face. At the cross, we can see what God was doing. Jesus described it like this:

> **John 3:16** *"For God so loved the world that He gave His only begotten Son, that whoever believes in Him should not perish but have everlasting life."*

At the foot of the cross, we have a whole different view of life. To live life without ever taking in that view means we miss the most important part of life. Think about it: Jesus' death is the most important part of your life! That is a powerfully truthful statement. This understanding is so true that without it, one misses out on the real life, the everlasting life, the more abundant life.

The Prodigal Parent

The cross is where we encounter the reality of sin and saving grace, the truth of mercy and hope, and the certainty of love so deep and wide that it is difficult— in fact, impossible—to comprehend! The cross is where we find hope and strength; it is where we come face to face with just how much God loves us and what Jesus did for us. At the foot of the cross, we see a Savior who was wounded because of our sins, bruised for us, punished instead of us—and who died that we might have life.

Think about how much money people spend to travel the world and see the sights. Think about how many people long to go on vacations and visit foreign lands. Think about how many pictures people collect to demonstrate the places they have visited. I want you to realize that none of those places can ever provide what the view from the foot of the cross can provide.

The Cross

At the cross, at the cross,
Where I first saw the light,
And the burden of my heart rolled away;
It was there by faith I received my sight,
And now I am happy all the day.

After visiting attractions, there may be pleasant memories, but there is no eternal, everlasting change. There may be a fleeting joy because one has seen the sights, but as time goes by, those memories eventually fade. There may be some happiness associated with the trip, but it will not be everlasting joy. However, when you take the journey to the foot of the cross, it will change you forever. It will change you forever and create an everlasting memory. There will be an unspeakable joy full of glory. The memory will not fade. Oh no, it will be just the opposite! It will grow day by day, week by week, and month by month.

The beauty of this journey will be everlasting. The impact on your life will be such, that you will never be the same. You will see with new eyes, dance with new feet, hear with new ears, and speak with a new voice. You will find a depth of understanding about who God is and who you are in God that it will be clear to you that you have been born again. You will find life has majorly shifted, and the most important thing to you will be what you discovered in that moment at the foot of the cross. When you look up and understand His sacrifice was made for you; when you comprehend that while Jesus was on the cross, you were on His mind—you will be changed forever!

One of the most somber and moving moments penned in the Bible captures Christ's words just hours before being nailed to the cross when Jesus predicts His death on the cross:

The Cross

> **John 12:27** *"Now My soul is troubled, and what shall I say? 'Father, save Me from this hour'? But for this purpose I came to this hour."*

Jesus, knowing He was about to face death and that death would be on the cross, strengthened Himself in prayer. He knew He was about to be wounded, bruised, beaten, and executed; He knew it was for this purpose that He came to this world.

> **John 12:32-33** *"And I, if I am lifted up from the earth, will draw all peoples to Myself." This He said, signifying by what death He would die.*

Without the cross, you and I would have no remedy for our sins. God, utilizing sinful men, led a sinless Savior to death on the cross. This He did to provide a way for sinners like you and me to be saved.

> **Hebrews 2:9** *But we see Jesus, who was made a little lower than the angels, for the suffering of death crowned with glory and honor, that He, by the grace of God, might taste death for everyone.*

> **Hebrews 9:28** *. . .so Christ was offered once to bear the sins of many.*

My beloved one, when you are standing at the foot of the cross, you realize that God the Father sent Jesus to humankind and allowed humankind to deliver Jesus, God the Son, to the cross. This would not have happened without the Father activating His plan and the Son obediently carrying out the plan.

The Cross

Philippians 2:8 *And being found in appearance as a man, He humbled Himself and became obedient to the point of death, even the death of the cross.*

Isaiah 53:10 *Yet it pleased the Lord to bruise Him; He has put Him to grief. When You make His soul an offering for sin. . . .*

God's purpose was that we might be made right in his sight, cleansed from our sins. Through Christ, our sins were punished, and we stand forgiven. God, being fair and just, would not punish both Christ and us for our sins; that would mean Jesus' death was in vain. God is love, and God has demonstrated this love in an undeniably spectacular fashion.

Romans 5:8 *But God demonstrates His own love*

toward us, in that while we were still sinners, Christ died for us.

There on the cross, God allowed Christ to become our sin substitute.

2 Corinthians 5:21 *For He made Him who knew no sin to be sin for us, that we might become the righteousness of God in Him.*

Now you might ask, "Why on earth would God do this?" My answer is that it is not on earth; it is love from above.

Ephesians 2:4-5 *But God, who is rich in mercy, because of His great love with which He loved us, even when we were dead in trespasses, made us alive together with Christ (by grace you have been saved). . ..*

The Cross

1 John 3:1 *Behold what manner of love the Father has bestowed on us, that we should be called children of God!*

I close this chapter with the very familiar scripture, spoken by Jesus Himself, which points us toward His wonderful sacrifice for us on the cross:

John 3:16 *"For God so loved the world that He gave His only begotten Son, that whoever believes in Him should not perish but have everlasting life."*

What I Should Have Taught You

The crucifixion of Jesus is a true historical event and was witnessed by many men and women. This is a statement of fact. Another fact is this: while Jesus was on the cross, you were on His mind! Yes, Jesus knew then that you would be here now. He knew you would need a Savior because He knew that you and I, as well as the rest of the world, would be sinful in our thoughts and deeds. The cross is where God demonstrated His great love for us! It is where God provided the perfect sacrifice for your sins and my sins.

Why did Jesus have to die for us? The answer is so that we may live for Him!

2 Corinthians 5:15 *. . .and He died for all, that those who live should live no longer for themselves, but for Him who died for them and rose again.*

2 Corinthians 5:21 *For He made Him who knew no sin to be sin for us, that we might become the righteousness of God in Him.*

The Cross

On the cross, God allowed Jesus to suffer and die in place of us. Oh, I want you to understand the view from the foot of the cross. I want you to look up and see the love that God poured out for you on the cross of Christ. I love you, and I want you to see, know, feel, and experience all the love that God poured out for you on the cross.

Jesus could have come down from the cross, but He stayed there and suffered and died. Please do not believe for a second that this was not a conscious choice on Jesus' part. Please think about the beauty of the following prayer, prayed by Jesus the night before He was arrested, falsely tried, and crucified:

> **Luke 22:41-42** *And He was withdrawn from them about a stone's throw, and He knelt down and prayed, saying, "Father, if it*

is Your will, take this cup away from Me; nevertheless not My will, but Yours, be done."

"Not My will, but Yours, be done." Jesus knew this hour would come, and He willingly faced the fate of the cross. He did this for you and me. He took upon Himself the punishment that we rightly deserved. One innocent life was traded for many sinful lives. Yes, dear one, Christ's death on the cross paid the price that we could never have paid ourselves.

My Prayer For You

My God and Father, I come to You now trusting and believing that You will hear and answer my prayer. I ask that You, by Your Holy Spirit, bring my beloved to the foot of the cross and allow her to take in the full beauty of that sacrifice. Lord, I ask

The Cross

that You open her eyes and understanding to see the depth, width, and height of the love You have for her. Father, I thank You that while Your Son and our Savior was on that cross, she was on His mind! Jesus, thank You for not coming down but fulfilling the will of the Father. Holy Spirit, I thank You for strengthening the Son to stay on the cross and for what You did in raising Him from the grave. Thank You for the resurrection power! It is in the name above all names, the blessed name of our Lord and Savior, Jesus the Christ, that I pray. Amen.

The Resurrection

1 Corinthians 15:14 *And if Christ is not risen, then our preaching is empty and your faith is also empty.*

My precious one, I have saved this portion for the end for this summarizes all that I need to communicate to you. If what has been written thus far makes you stop and ponder those things I should have taught you, then this is the final point that must be put in front of you. The resurrection of Jesus Christ is central to all that I have written. Therefore, you must wrestle with this thought:

The Resurrection

What do YOU do with the Resurrected Jesus?

This Resurrected Jesus, He who was once dead but who is now alive, of necessity becomes the reality with which all humankind must grapple. The Resurrected Jesus, who was crucified on the cross but now lives, is a truth that you must resolve in your own heart. What is your relationship to this Resurrected Jesus?

> **Romans 10:9** . . .*that if you confess with your mouth the Lord Jesus and believe in your heart that God has raised Him from the dead, you will be saved.*

You see, my dear, it is one thing to say you believe in God; it is another thing altogether to believe the Lord Jesus, God's only son, came and died for our sins and rose from the dead. Once that belief takes root and becomes reality, the Bible states you will be saved. That reality, the fact that God raised Him from the dead, means that everyone must resolve their own relationship with Jesus.

The truth of His resurrection is supported in the words of the Bible; in fact, there were eyewitnesses:

> **Acts 2:32** *"This Jesus God has raised up, of which we are all witnesses."*

> **1 Corinthians 15:3-8** *For I delivered to you first of all that which I also received: that Christ died for our sins according to the Scriptures, and that He was buried, and that He rose again the third day according to the Scriptures, and that He was seen by Cephas, then by the twelve.*

The Resurrection

After that He was seen by over five hundred brethren at once, of whom the greater part remain to the present, but some have fallen asleep. After that He was seen by James, then by all the apostles. Then last of all He was seen by me also, as by one born out of due time.

The Bible clearly communicates there were those who saw the Resurrected Jesus, those who spoke with Him, and even those who touched Him:

John 20:24-29 *Now Thomas, called the Twin, one of the twelve, was not with them when Jesus came. The other disciples therefore said to him, "We have seen the Lord."*

So he said to them, "Unless I see in His hands the print of the nails, and put my finger into the print of the nails, and put my hand into His side, I will not believe."

And after eight days His disciples were again inside, and Thomas with them. Jesus came, the doors being shut, and stood in the midst, and said, "Peace to you!" Then He said to Thomas, "Reach your finger here, and look at My hands; and reach your hand here, and put it into My side. Do not be unbelieving, but believing."

And Thomas answered and said to Him, "My Lord and my God!"

Jesus said to him, "Thomas, because you have seen Me, you have believed. <u>Blessed are those who have not seen and yet have believed.</u>"

The Resurrection

Look at the last words in the excerpt above: *"<u>Blessed are those who have not seen and yet have believed.</u>"* Therein lies the key to understanding how belief works: *"those who have not seen. . .yet have believed."* This would be impossible without God intervening within the heart of a man or a woman. The fact that a person believes is because God gives her the power to believe. God has made it real to her, and she has accepted the fact of the Resurrected Jesus by faith.

The Resurrected Jesus came back to Thomas and said, *"Do not be unbelieving, but believing"* because He chose Thomas. Jesus will also make Himself known to all who belong to Him, all whom He chooses.

Dear one, that tugging feeling in your heart is the Lord pulling you toward Him. He is increasing your faith and making the reality of the resurrection of Jesus your

The Prodigal Parent

reality! He wants you to cry out just as Thomas did: *"My Lord and my God!"*

Precious one, the whole world must deal with the Resurrected Jesus by either accepting Him or rejecting Him; there is no in-between.

It is a fact that Jesus was raised from the dead, and we have a living Savior. This is a statement of fact for every true born-again believer. The place of belief is in the heart. There must be a deep internal belief that Jesus is alive, and because He lives, He provides the hope needed to navigate this life and bring us safely to the shores of the next life—the eternal life. Not only that, but in this present life, Jesus wants us to experience and live an abundant life. It is because of Him that we find our joy and hope in this life because we know we have received eternal life.

The Resurrection

What I Should Have Taught You

Jesus is the risen Lord. He died on the cross for your sins and my sins.

But that's not the end of the story. He rose again, and He is the living Christ! Yes, Christ is alive! If Christ is not alive, there is no hope for any of us. But He is alive! And Scripture says:

> **Romans 10:9** . . .*that if you confess with your mouth the Lord Jesus and believe in your heart that God has raised Him from the dead, you will be saved.*

The fact that we have a resurrected Savior forces everyone to deal with the reality of facing that resurrected Savior. The question becomes, as an individual, are you ready to face the resurrected Savior? Are you among those who have

The Prodigal Parent

received the blessing that the Resurrected Jesus spoke to his disciple?

> **John 20:29** *Jesus said to him, "Thomas, because you have seen Me, you have believed. Blessed are those who have not seen and yet have believed."*

Jesus made himself known to Thomas because Thomas doubted the fact that Jesus had risen from the dead. He showed Thomas the wounds He had received by being nailed to the cross and pierced in the side by a sword:

> **John 20:27** *Then He said to Thomas, "Reach your finger here, and look at My hands; and reach your hand here, and put it into My side. Do not be unbelieving, but believing."*

The Resurrection

Jesus knows everyone who belongs to Him. Just like He made Himself known to Thomas, He will make Himself known to all who believe.

Jesus rose from the dead, and one day, we who believe will be with Him:

> **John 14:1-3** *"Let not your heart be troubled; you believe in God, believe also in Me. In My Father's house are many mansions; if it were not so, I would have told you. I go to prepare a place for you. And if I go and prepare a place for you, I will come again and receive you to Myself; that where I am, there you may be also."*

Because Christ rose from the dead, He gained a decisive victory over death and over sin, and we no longer need to fear death. Jesus said, *"I go to prepare a place for you."* <u>This earth is not our home!</u>

Because Christ rose from the dead, we know that God has accepted His sacrificial death and has forgiven our sins.

Because Christ rose from the dead, we know there is life after death, and if we belong to Him, we need not fear death or hell:

> **John 11:25-26** *Jesus said to her, "I am the resurrection and the life. He who believes in Me, though he may die, he shall live. And whoever lives and believes in Me shall never die. Do you believe this?"*

We know these words are true because Jesus died on the cross and rose again from the dead. What a glorious hope we have because of Jesus' resurrection!

> **John 6:35-40** *And Jesus said to them, "I am the bread of life. He who comes to Me shall never hunger, and he who believes in Me shall never thirst. But I said to you that you have seen Me and yet do not believe. All that the Father gives Me will come to Me, and the one who comes to Me I will by no means cast out. For I have come down from heaven, not to do My own will, but the will of Him who sent Me.*
>
> *"This is the will of the Father who sent Me, that of all He has given Me I should lose nothing, but should raise it up at the last day. And this is the will of Him who sent Me, that everyone who sees the Son and believes in Him*

may have everlasting life; and I will raise him up at the last day."

My Prayer For You

My God and my Father, once again I come before You, trusting and believing that You hear my prayer. I pray that You will open the heart of my beloved and allow the reality of the resurrection of Jesus Christ to take deep and full root in the fertile soil of her heart. I pray that You will make it a daily reality for her to know and understand the depth, width, and height of the love which You have for her. I pray for the blessed truth of the resurrection to be a light that shines in her life. Lord, I ask You to make it known to her so she may cry out just as Thomas did: *"My Lord and my God!"* I ask this in the name above all names, in the name of the resurrected Savior, in Jesus' name. Amen.

End Matters

I have prayed for God to guide every word that is contained in this book. I am trusting Him to speak to you through this writing.

- I can trust Him for this because I have trusted Him to be the Savior of my soul.
- I can trust Him for this because my life has been changed forever through my relationship with God the Father; God the Son, Jesus; and God the Holy Spirit.
- I can trust Him to speak to you because His word, as recorded in the Bible, was written for you and to you.

- I can trust Him because I have prayed for you and asked Him to draw you to Him.
- I can trust Him because I have prayed and asked God to bless you, watch over you, and keep you from hurt, danger, and harm.
- I have prayed and continue to pray that God will grant you access to Him through a strong and effectual prayer life.
- I have prayed that God will guide you to fulfill His plan and purpose in your life.
- I have prayed for Him to bring you into that abundant life He has promised.
- I have prayed and asked God to stir up the gifts that He has given you and to use you for His kingdom.
- I have prayed and asked God to draw you into His service so that you may be used for His glory!

End Matters

I believe God has heard my prayers, and I believe He has GREAT things planned for you. This verse from *The Message Bible* reinforces my belief:

> **Jeremiah 29:11** *I know what I'm doing. I have it all planned out—plans to take care of you, not abandon you, plans to give you the future you hope for.*

This is a promise from God to those who belong to Him. This is the great thing that we who belong to the Lord have working for us! Although we will face difficult times, we can trust that God is working for our good and His glory.

> **Romans 8:28** *And we know that all things work together for good to those who love God, to those who are the called according to His purpose.*

The Prodigal Parent

What the Lord wants from us is that we trust Him and look exclusively to Him to be the fulfillment in our lives.

> **Proverbs 3:5-6** *Trust in the Lord with all your heart, And lean not on your own understanding; In all your ways acknowledge Him, And He shall direct your paths.*

I love you now and forever!

8/1/23 - Father, I do trust you!
I trust you w/ my children,
their children -

I'm looking to you for guidance
w/ them - I pray earnestly
that they will come back to you -
that they will desire you to be
the center of their lives -
that they will come to know
the height, width, depth of
your love for them.

And I pray they will
enjoy eternal life!

Thank you - Love,
a mom that has the
biggest ♡ for her fam

CPSIA information can be obtained
at www.ICGtesting.com
Printed in the USA
BVHW081552100323
660176BV00005B/328